Hard Press

LETTERS TO HIS SON

1746-1747

By the EARL OF CHESTERFIELD

SPECIAL INTRODUCTION

The proud Lord Chesterfield would have turned in his grave had he known that he was to go down to posterity as a teacher and preacher of the gospel of not grace, but—"the graces, the graces, the graces." Natural gifts, social status, open opportunities, and his ambition, all conspired to destine him for high statesmanship. If anything was lacking in his qualifications, he had the pluck and good sense to work hard and persistently until the deficiency was made up. Something remained lacking, and not all his consummate mastery of arts could conceal that conspicuous want,—the want of heart.

Teacher and preacher he assuredly is, and long will be, yet no thanks are his due from a posterity of the common people whom he so sublimely despised. His pious mission was not to raise the level of the multitude, but to lift a single individual upon a pedestal so high that his lowly origin should not betray itself. That individual was his, Lord Chesterfield's, illegitimate son, whose inferior blood should be given the true blue hue by concentrating upon him all the externals of aristocratic education.

Never had pupil so devoted, persistent, lavish, and brilliant a guide, philosopher, and friend, for the parental relation was shrewdly merged in these. Never were devotion and uphill struggle against doubts of success more bitterly repaid. Philip Stanhope was born in 1732, when his father was thirty-eight. He absorbed readily enough the solids of the ideal education supplied him, but, by perversity of fate, he cared not a fig for "the graces, the graces, the graces," which his father so wisely deemed by far the superior qualities to be cultivated by the budding courtier and statesman. A few years of minor services to his country were rendered, though Chesterfield was breaking his substitute for a heart because his son could not or would not play the superfine gentleman—on the paternal model, and then came the news of his death, when only thirty-six. What was a still greater shock to the lordly father, now deaf, gouty, fretful, and at outs with the world, his informant reported that she had been secretly married for several years to Young Hopeful, and was left penniless with two boys. Lord Chesterfield was above all things a practical philosopher, as hard and as exquisitely rounded and polished as a granite column. He accepted the vanishing of his lifelong dream with the admirable stolidity of a fatalist, and in those last days of his radically artificial life he disclosed a welcome tenderness, a touch of the divine, none the less so for being common duty, shown in the few brief letters to his son's widow and to "our boys." This, and his enviable gift of being able to view the downs as well as the ups of life in the consoling humorous light, must modify the sterner judgment so easily passed upon his characteristic inculcation, if not practice, of heartlessness.

The thirteenth-century mother church in the town from which Lord Chesterfield's title came has a peculiar steeple, graceful in its lines, but it points askew, from whatever quarter it is seen. The writer of these Letters, which he never dreamed would be published, is the best self-portrayed Gentleman in literature. In everything he was naturally a stylist, perfected by assiduous art, yet the graceful steeple is somehow warped out of the beauty of the perpendicular. His ideal Gentleman is the frigid product of a rigid mechanical drill, with the mien of a posture master, the skin-deep graciousness of a French Marechal, the calculating adventurer who cuts unpretentious worthies to toady to society magnates, who affects the supercilious air of a shallow dandy and cherishes the heart of a frog. True, he repeatedly insists on the obligation of truthfulness in all things, and of, honor in dealing with the world. His Gentleman may; nay, he must, sail with the stream, gamble in moderation if it is the fashion, must stoop to wear ridiculous clothes and ornaments if they are the mode, though despising his weakness all to himself, and no true Gentleman could afford to keep out of the little gallantries which so effectively advertised him as a man of spirit sad charm. Those repeated injunctions of honor are to be the rule, subject to these exceptions, which transcend the common proprieties when the subject is the rising young gentleman of the period and his goal social success. If an undercurrent of shady morality is traceable in this Chesterfieldian philosophy it must, of course, be explained away by the less perfect moral standard of his period as compared with that of our day. Whether this holds strictly true of men may be open to discussion, but his lordship's worldly instructions as to the utility of women as stepping-stones to favor in high places are equally at variance with the principles he so impressively inculcates and with modern conceptions of social honor. The externals of good breeding cannot be over-estimated, if honestly come by, nor is it necessary to examine too deeply into the prime motives of those who urge them upon a generation in whose eyes matter is more important than manner. Superficial refinement is better than none, but the Chesterfield pulpit cannot afford to shirk the duty of proclaiming loud and far that the only courtesy worthy of respect is that 'politesse de coeur,' the politeness of the heart, which finds expression in consideration for others as the ruling principle of conduct. This militates to some extent against the assumption of fine airs without the backing of fine behavior, and if it tends to discourage the effort to use others for selfish ends, it nevertheless pays better in the long run.

Chesterfield's frankness in so many confessions of sharp practice almost merits his canonization as a minor saint of society. Dr. Johnson has indeed placed him on a Simeon Stylites pillar, an immortality of penance from which no good member of the writers' guild is likely to pray his deliverance. He commends the fine art and high science of dissimulation with the gusto of an apostle and the authority of an expert. Dissimulate, but do not simulate, disguise your real sentiments, but do not falsify them. Go through the world with your eyes and ears open and mouth mostly shut. When new or stale gossip is brought to you, never let on that you know it already, nor that it really interests you. The reading of these Letters is better than hearing the average comedy, in which the wit of a single sentence of Chesterfield suffices to carry an act. His man-of-the-world philosophy is as old as the Proverbs of Solomon, but will always be fresh and true, and enjoyable at any age, thanks to his pithy expression, his unfailing common sense, his sparkling wit and charming humor. This latter gift shows in the seeming lapses from his rigid rule requiring absolute elegance of expression at all times, when an unexpected coarseness, in some provincial colloquialism, crops out with picturesque force. The beau ideal of superfineness occasionally enjoys the bliss of harking back to mother English.

Above all the defects that can be charged against the Letters, there rises the substantial merit of an honest effort to exalt the gentle in woman and man—above the merely genteel. "He that is gentil doeth gentil deeds," runs the mediaeval saying which marks the distinction between the genuine and the sham in behavior. A later age had it thus: "Handsome is as handsome does," and in this larger sense we have agreed to accept the motto of William of Wykeham, which declares that "Manners maketh Man." *Oliver* H. G. *Leigh*

LETTER I

Bath, October 9, O. S. 1746

Dear boy: Your distresses in your journey from Heidelberg to Schaffhausen, your lying upon straw, your black bread, and your broken 'berline,' are proper seasonings for the greater fatigues and distresses which you must expect in the course of your travels; and, if one had a mind to moralize, one might call them the samples of the accidents, rubs, and difficulties, which every man meets with in his journey through life. In this journey, the understanding is the 'voiture' that must carry you through; and in proportion as that is stronger or weaker, more or less in repair, your journey will be better or worse; though at best you will now and then find some bad roads, and some bad inns. Take care, therefore, to keep that necessary 'voiture' in perfect good repair; examine, improve, and strengthen it every day: it is in the power, and ought to be the care, of every man to do it; he that neglects it, deserves to feel, and certainly will feel, the fatal effects of that negligence.

'A propos' of negligence: I must say something to you upon that subject. You know I have often told you, that my affection for you was not a weak, womanish one; and, far from blinding me, it makes me but more quick-sighted as to your faults; those it is not only my right, but my duty to tell you of; and it is your duty and your interest to correct them. In the strict scrutiny which I have made into you, I have (thank God) hitherto not discovered any vice of the heart, or any peculiar weakness of the head: but I have discovered laziness, inattention, and indifference; faults which are only pardonable in old men, who, in the decline of life, when health and spirits fail, have a kind of claim to that sort of tranquillity. But a young man should be ambitious to shine, and excel; alert, active, and indefatigable in the means of doing it; and, like Cæsar, 'Nil actum reputans, si quid superesset agendum.' You seem to want that 'vivida vis animi,' which spurs and excites most young men to please, to shine, to excel. Without the desire and the pains necessary to be considerable, depend upon it, you never can be so; as, without the desire and attention necessary to please, you never can please. 'Nullum numen abest, si sit prudentia,' is unquestionably true, with regard to everything except poetry; and I am very sure that any man of common understanding may, by proper culture, care, attention, and labor, make himself whatever he pleases, except a good poet. Your destination is the great and busy world; your immediate object is the affairs, the interests, and the history, the constitutions, the customs, and the manners of the several parts of Europe. In this, any man of common sense may, by common application, be sure to excel. Ancient and modern history are, by attention, easily attainable. Geography and chronology the same, none of them requiring any uncommon share of genius or invention. Speaking and Writing, clearly, correctly, and with ease and grace, are certainly to be acquired, by reading the best authors with care, and by attention to the best living models. These are the qualifications more particularly necessary for you, in your department, which you may be possessed of, if you please; and which, I tell you fairly, I shall be very angry at you, if you are not; because, as you have the means in your hands, it will be your own fault only.

If care and application are necessary to the acquiring of those qualifications, without which you can never be considerable, nor make a figure in the world, they are not less necessary with regard to the lesser accomplishments, which are requisite to make you agreeable and pleasing in society. In truth, whatever is worth doing at all, is worth doing well; and nothing can be done well without attention: I therefore carry the necessity of attention down to the lowest things, even to dancing and dress. Custom has made dancing sometimes necessary for a young man; therefore mind it while you learn it that you may learn to do it well, and not be ridiculous, though in a ridiculous act. Dress is of the same nature; you must dress; therefore attend to it; not in order to rival or to excel a fop in it, but in order to avoid singularity, and consequently ridicule. Take great care always to be dressed like the reasonable people of your own age, in the place where you are; whose dress is never spoken of one way or another, as either too negligent or too much studied.

What is commonly called an absent man, is commonly either a very weak, or a very affected man; but be he which he will, he is, I am sure, a very disagreeable man in company. He fails in all the common offices of civility; he seems not to know those people to-day, whom yesterday he appeared to live in intimacy with. He takes no part in the general conversation; but, on the contrary, breaks into it from time to time, with some start of his own, as if he waked from a dream. This (as I said before) is a sure indication, either of a mind so weak that it is not able to bear above one object at a time; or so affected, that it would be supposed to be wholly engrossed by, and directed to, some very great and important objects. Sir Isaac Newton, Mr. Locke, and (it may be) five or six more, since the creation of the world, may have had a right to absence, from that intense thought which the things they were investigating required. But if a young man, and a man of the world, who has no such avocations to plead, will claim and exercise that right of absence in company, his pretended right should, in my mind, be turned into an involuntary absence, by his perpetual exclusion out of company. However frivolous a company may be, still, while you are among them, do not show them, by your inattention, that you think them so; but rather take their tone, and conform in some degree to their weakness, instead of manifesting your contempt for them. There is nothing that people bear more impatiently, or forgive less, than contempt; and an injury is much sooner forgotten than an insult. If, therefore, you would rather please than offend, rather be well than ill spoken of, rather be loved than hated; remember to have that constant attention about you which flatters every man's little vanity; and the want of which, by mortifying his pride, never fails to excite his resentment, or at least his ill will. For instance, most people (I might say all people) have their weaknesses; they have their aversions and their likings, to such or such things; so that, if you were to laugh at a man for his aversion to a cat, or cheese (which are common antipathies), or, by inattention and negligence, to let them come in his way, where you could prevent it, he would, in the first case, think himself insulted, and, in the second, slighted, and would remember both. Whereas your care to procure for him what he likes, and to remove from him what he hates, shows him that he is at least an object of your attention; flatters his vanity, and makes him possibly more your friend, than a more important service would have done. With regard to women, attentions still below these are necessary, and, by the custom of the world, in some measure due, according to the laws of good-breeding.

My long and frequent letters, which I send you, in great doubt of their success, put me in mind of certain papers, which you have very lately, and I formerly, sent up to kites, along the string, which we called messengers; some of them the wind used to blow away, others were torn by the string, and but few of them got up and stuck to the kite. But I will content myself now, as I did then, if some of my present messengers do but stick to you. Adieu!

LETTER II

Dear boy: You are by this time (I suppose) quite settled and at home at Lausanne; therefore pray let me know how you pass your time there, and what your studies, your amusements, and your acquaintances are. I take it for granted, that you inform yourself daily of the nature of the government and constitution of the Thirteen Cantons; and as I am ignorant of them myself, must apply to you for information. I know the names, but I do not know the nature of some of the most considerable offices there; such as the Avoyers, the Seizeniers, the Banderets, and the Gros Sautier. I desire, therefore, that you will let me know what is the particular business, department, or province of these several magistrates. But as I imagine that there may be some, though, I believe, no essential difference, in the governments of the several Cantons, I would not give you the trouble of informing yourself of each of them; but confine my inquiries, as you may your informations, to the Canton you reside in, that of Berne, which I take to be the principal one. I am not sure whether the Pays de Vaud, where you are, being a conquered country, and taken from the Dukes of Savoy, in the year 1536, has the same share in the government of the Canton, as the German part of it has. Pray inform yourself and me about it.

I have this moment received yours from Berne, of the 2d October, N. S. and also one from Mr. Harte, of the same date, under Mr. Burnaby's cover. I find by the latter, and indeed I thought so before, that some of your letters and some of Mr. Harte's have not reached me. Wherefore, for the future, I desire, that both he and you will direct your letters for me, to be left chés Monsieur Wolters, Agent de S. M. Britanique, a Rotterdam, who will take care to send them to me safe. The reason why you have not received letters either from me or from Grevenkop was that we directed them to Lausanne, where we thought you long ago: and we thought it to no purpose to direct to you upon your *Route*, where it was little likely that our letters would meet with you. But you have, since your arrival at Lausanne, I believe, found letters enough from me; and it may be more than you have read, at least with attention.

I am glad that you like Switzerland so well; and am impatient to hear how other matters go, after your settlement at Lausanne. God bless you!

LETTER III

London, December 2, O.S. 1746.

Dear boy: I have not, in my present situation,—[His Lordship was, in the year 1746, appointed one of his Majesty's secretaries of state.]—time to write to you, either so much or so often as I used, while I was in a place of much more leisure and profit; but my affection for you must not be judged of by the number of my letters; and, though the one lessens, the other, I assure you, does not.

I have just now received your letter of the 25th past, N. S., and, by the former post, one from Mr. Harte; with both which I am very well pleased: with Mr. Harte's, for the good account which he gives me of you; with yours, for the good account which you gave me of what I desired to be informed of. Pray continue to give me further information of the form of government of the country you are now in; which I hope you will know most minutely before you leave it. The inequality of the town of Lausanne seems to be very convenient in this cold weather; because going up hill and down will keep you warm. You say there is a good deal of good company; pray, are you got into it? Have you made acquaintances, and with whom? Let me know some of their names. Do you learn German yet, to read, write, and speak it?

Yesterday, I saw a letter from Monsieur Bochat to a friend of mine; which gave me the greatest pleasure that I have felt this great while; because it gives so very good an account of you. Among other things which Monsieur Bochat says to your advantage, he mentions the tender uneasiness and concern that you showed during my illness, for which (though I will say that you owe it to me) I am obliged to you: sentiments of gratitude not being universal, nor even common. As your affection for me can only proceed from your experience and conviction of my fondness for you (for to talk of natural affection is talking nonsense), the only return I desire is, what it is chiefly your interest to make me; I mean your invariable practice of virtue, and your indefatigable pursuit of knowledge. Adieu! and be persuaded that I shall love you extremely, while you deserve it; but not one moment longer.

LETTER IV

London, December 9, O. S. 1746.

Dear boy: Though I have very little time, and though I write by this post to Mr. Harte, yet I cannot send a packet to Lausanne without a word or two to yourself. I thank you for your letter of congratulation which you wrote me, notwithstanding the pain it gave you. The accident that caused the pain was, I presume, owing to that degree of giddiness, of which I have sometimes taken the liberty to speak to you. The post I am now in, though the object of most people's views and desires, was in some degree inflicted upon me; and a certain concurrence of circumstances obliged me to engage in it. But I feel that to go through with it requires more strength of body and mind than I have: were you three or four years older; you should share in my trouble, and I would have taken you into my office; but I hope you will employ these three or four years so well as to make yourself capable of being of use to me, if I should continue in it so long. The reading, writing, and speaking the modern languages correctly; the knowledge of the laws of nations, and the particular constitution of the empire; of history, geography, and chronology, are absolutely necessary to this business, for which I have always intended you. With these qualifications you may very possibly be my successor, though not my immediate one.

I hope you employ your whole time, which few people do; and that you put every moment to, profit of some kind or other. I call company, walking, riding, *etc.*, employing one's time, and, upon proper occasions, very usefully; but what I cannot forgive in anybody is sauntering, and doing nothing at all, with a thing so precious as time, and so irrecoverable when lost.

Are you acquainted with any ladies at Lausanne? and do you behave yourself with politeness enough to make them desire your company?

I must finish: God bless you!

LETTER V

London, February 24, O. S. 1747

Sir: In order that we may, reciprocally, keep up our French, which, for want of practice, we might forget; you will permit me to have the honor of assuring you of my respects in that language: and be so good to answer me in the same. Not that I am apprehensive of your forgetting to speak French: since it is probable that two-thirds of our daily prattle is in that language; and because, if you leave off writing French, you may perhaps neglect that grammatical purity, and accurate orthography, which, in other languages, you excel in; and really, even in French, it is better to write well than ill. However, as this is a language very proper for sprightly, gay subjects, I shall conform to that, and reserve those which are serious for English. I shall not therefore mention to you, at present, your Greek or Latin, your study of the Law of Nature, or the Law of Nations, the Rights of People, or of Individuals; but rather discuss the subject of your Amusements and Pleasures; for, to say the truth, one must have some. May I be permitted to inquire of what nature yours are? Do they consist in little commercial play at cards in good company? are they little agreeable suppers, at which cheerfulness and decency are united? or, do you pay court to some fair one, who requires such attentions as may be of use in contributing to polish you? Make me your confidant upon this subject; you shall not find a severe censor: on the contrary, I wish to obtain the employment of minister to your pleasures: I will point them out, and even contribute to them.

Many young people adopt pleasures, for which they have not the least taste, only because they are called by that name. They often mistake so totally, as to imagine that debauchery is pleasure. You must allow that drunkenness, which is equally destructive to body and mind, is a fine pleasure. Gaming, that draws you into a thousand scrapes, leaves you penniless, and gives you the air and manners of an outrageous madman, is another most exquisite pleasure; is it not? As to running after women, the consequences of that vice are only the loss of one's nose, the total destruction of health, and, not unfrequently, the being run through the body.

These, you see, are all trifles; yet this is the catalogue of pleasures of most of those young people, who never reflecting themselves, adopt, indiscriminately, what others choose to call by the seducing name of pleasure. I am thoroughly persuaded you will not fall into such errors; and that, in the choice of your amusements, you will be directed by reason, and a discerning taste. The true pleasures of a gentleman are those of the table, but within the bound of moderation; good company, that is to say, people of merit; moderate play, which amuses, without any interested views; and sprightly gallant conversations with women of fashion and sense.

These are the real pleasures of a gentleman; which occasion neither sickness, shame, nor repentance. Whatever exceeds them, becomes low vice, brutal passion, debauchery, and insanity of, mind; all of which, far from giving satisfaction, bring on dishonor and disgrace. Adieu.

LETTER VI

London, March 6, O. S. 1747

Dear boy: Whatever you do, will always affect me, very sensibly, one way or another; and I am now most agreeably affected, by two letters, which I have lately seen from Lausanne, upon your subject; the one from Madame St. Germain, the other from Monsieur Pampigny: they both give so good an account of you, that I thought myself obliged, in justice both to them and, to you, to let you know it. Those who deserve a good character, ought to have the satisfaction of knowing that they have it, both as a reward and as an encouragement. They write, that you are not only 'decrotte,' but tolerably well-bred; and that the English crust of awkward bashfulness, shyness, and roughness (of which, by the bye, you had your share) is pretty well rubbed off. I am most heartily glad of it; for, as I have often told you, those lesser talents, of an engaging, insinuating manner, an easy good-breeding, a genteel behavior and address, are of infinitely more advantage than they are generally thought to be, especially here in England. Virtue and learning, like gold, have their intrinsic value but if they are not polished, they certainly lose a great deal of their luster; and even polished brass will pass upon more people than rough gold. What a number of sins does the cheerful, easy good-breeding of the French frequently cover? Many of them want common sense, many more common learning; but in general, they make up so much by their manner, for those defects, that frequently they pass undiscovered: I have often said, and do think, that a Frenchman, who, with a fund of virtue, learning and good sense, has the manners and good-breeding of his country, is the perfection of human nature. This perfection you may, if you please, and I hope you will, arrive at. You know what virtue is: you may have it if you will; it is in every man's power; and miserable is the man who has it not. Good sense God has given you. Learning you already possess enough of, to have, in a reasonable time, all that a man need have. With this, you are thrown out early into the world, where it will be your own fault if you do not acquire all, the other accomplishments necessary to complete and adorn your character. You will do well to make your compliments to Madame St. Germain and Monsieur Pampigny; and tell them, how sensible you are of their partiality to you, in the advantageous testimonies which, you are informed, they have given of you here.

Adieu. Continue to deserve such testimonies; and then you will not only deserve, but enjoy my truest affection.

LETTER VII

London, March 27, O. S. 1747.

Dear boy: Pleasure is the rock which most young people split upon: they launch out with crowded sails in quest of it, but without a compass to direct their course, or reason sufficient to steer the vessel; for want of which, pain and shame, instead of pleasure, are the returns of their voyage. Do not think that I mean to snarl at pleasure, like a Stoic, or to preach against it, like a parson; no, I mean to point it out, and recommend it to you, like an Epicurean: I wish you a great deal; and my only view is to hinder you from mistaking it.

The character which most young men first aim at, is that of a man of pleasure; but they generally take it upon trust; and instead of consulting their own taste and inclinations, they blindly adopt whatever those with whom they chiefly converse, are pleased to call by the name of pleasure; and a man of pleasure in the vulgar acceptation of that phrase, means only, a beastly drunkard, an abandoned whoremaster, and a profligate swearer and curser. As it may be of use to you, I am not unwilling, though at the same time ashamed to own, that the vices of my youth proceeded much more from my silly resolution of being, what I heard called a man of pleasure, than from my own inclinations. I always naturally hated drinking; and yet I have often drunk; with disgust at the time, attended by great sickness the next day, only because I then considered drinking as a necessary qualification for a fine gentleman, and a man of pleasure.

The same as to gaming. I did not want money, and consequently had no occasion to play for it; but I thought play another necessary ingredient in the composition of a man of pleasure, and accordingly I plunged into it without desire, at first; sacrificed a thousand real pleasures to it; and made myself solidly uneasy by it, for thirty the best years of my life.

I was even absurd enough, for a little while, to swear, by way of adorning and completing the shining character which I affected; but this folly I soon laid aside, upon finding berth the guilt and the indecency of it.

Thus seduced by fashion, and blindly adopting nominal pleasures, I lost real ones; and my fortune impaired, and my constitution shattered, are, I must confess, the just punishment of my errors.

Take warning then by them: choose your pleasures for yourself, and do not let them be imposed upon you. Follow nature and not fashion: weigh the present enjoyment of your pleasures against the necessary consequences of them, and then let your own common sense determine your choice.

Were I to begin the world again, with the experience which I now have of it, I would lead a life of real, not of imaginary pleasures. I would enjoy the pleasures of the table, and of wine; but stop short of the pains inseparably annexed to an excess of either. I would not, at twenty years, be a preaching missionary of abstemiousness and sobriety; and I should let other people do as they would, without formally and sententiously rebuking them for it; but I would be most firmly resolved not to destroy my own faculties and constitution; in complaisance to those who have no regard to their own. I would play to give me pleasure, but not to give me pain; that is, I would play for trifles, in mixed companies, to amuse myself, and conform to custom; but I would take care not to venture for sums; which, if I won, I should not be the better for; but, if I lost, should be under a difficulty to pay: and when paid, would oblige me to retrench in several other articles. Not to mention the quarrels which deep play commonly occasions.

I would pass some of my time in reading, and the rest in the company of people of sense and learning, and chiefly those above me; and I would frequent the mixed companies of men and women of fashion, which, though often frivolous, yet they unbend and refresh the mind, not uselessly, because they certainly polish and soften the manners.

These would be my pleasures and amusements, if I were to live the last thirty years over again; they are rational ones; and, moreover, I will tell you, they are really the fashionable ones; for the others are not, in truth, the pleasures of what I call people of fashion, but of those who only call themselves so. Does good company care to have a man reeling drunk among them? Or to see another tearing his hair, and blaspheming, for having lost, at play, more than he is able to pay? Or a whoremaster with half a nose, and crippled by coarse and infamous debauchery? No; those who practice, and much more those who brag of them, make no part of good company; and are most unwillingly, if ever, admitted into it. A real man of fashion and pleasures observes decency: at least neither borrows nor affects vices: and if he unfortunately has any, he gratifies them with choice, delicacy, and secrecy.

I have not mentioned the pleasures of the mind (which are the solid and permanent ones); because they do not come under the head of what people commonly call pleasures; which they seem to confine to the senses. The pleasure of virtue, of charity, and of learning is true and lasting pleasure; with which I hope you will be well and long acquainted. Adieu!

LETTER VIII

London, April 3, O. S. 1747

Dear boy: If I am rightly informed, I am now writing to a fine gentleman, in a scarlet coat laced with gold, a brocade waistcoat, and all other suitable ornaments. The natural partiality of every author for his own works makes me very glad to hear that Mr. Harte has thought this last edition of mine worth so fine a binding; and, as he has bound it in red, and gilt it upon the back, I hope he will take care that it shall be *lettered* too. A showish binding attracts the eyes, and engages the attention of everybody; but with this difference, that women, and men who are like women, mind the binding more than the book; whereas men of sense and learning immediately examine the inside; and if they find that it does not answer the finery on the outside, they throw it by with the greater indignation and contempt. I hope that, when this edition of my works shall be opened and read, the best judges will find connection, consistency, solidity, and spirit in it. Mr. Harte may 'recensere' and 'emendare,' as much as he pleases; but it will be to little purpose, if you do not cooperate with him. The work will be imperfect.

I thank you for your last information of our success in the Mediterranean, and you say very rightly that a secretary of state ought to be well informed. I hope, therefore, you will take care that I shall. You are near the busy scene in Italy; and I doubt not but that, by frequently looking at the map, you have all that theatre of the war very perfect in your mind.

I like your account of the salt works; which shows that you gave some attention while you were seeing them. But notwithstanding that, by your account, the Swiss salt is (I dare say) very good, yet I am apt to suspect that it falls a little short of the true Attic salt in which there was a peculiar quickness and delicacy. That same Attic salt seasoned almost all Greece, except Boeotia, and a great deal of it was exported afterward to Rome, where it was counterfeited by a composition called Urbanity, which in some time was brought to very near the perfection of the original Attic salt. The more you are powdered with these two kinds of salt, the better you will keep, and the more you will be relished.

Adieu! My compliments to Mr. Harte and Mr. Eliot.

LETTER IX

London, April 14, O. S. 1747.

Dear boy: If you feel half the pleasure from the consciousness of doing well, that I do from the informations I have lately received in your favor from Mr. Harte, I shall have little occasion to exhort or admonish you any more to do what your own satisfaction and self love will sufficiently prompt you to. Mr. Harte tells me that you attend, that you apply to your studies; and that beginning to understand, you begin to taste them. This pleasure will increase, and keep pace with your attention; so that the balance will be greatly to your advantage. You may remember, that I have always earnestly recommended to you, to do what you are about, be that what it will; and to do nothing else at the same time. Do not imagine that I mean by this, that you should attend to and plod at your book all day long; far from it; I mean that you should have your pleasures too; and that you should attend to them for the time; as much as to your studies; and, if you do not attend equally to both, you will neither have improvement nor satisfaction from either. A man is fit for neither business nor pleasure, who either cannot, or does not, command and direct his attention to the present object, and, in some degree, banish for that time all other objects from his thoughts. If at a ball, a supper, or a party of pleasure, a man were to be solving, in his own mind, a problem in Euclid, he would be a very bad companion, and make a very poor figure in that company; or if, in studying a problem in his closet, he were to think of a minuet, I am apt to believe that he would make a very poor mathematician. There is time enough for everything, in the course of the day, if you do but one thing at once; but there is not time enough in the year, if you will do two things at a time. The Pensionary de Witt, who was torn to pieces in the year 1672, did the whole business of the Republic, and yet had time left to go to assemblies in the evening, and sup in company. Being asked how he could possibly find time to go through so much business, and yet amuse himself in the evenings as he did, he answered, there was nothing so easy; for that it was only doing one thing at a time, and never putting off anything till to-morrow that could be done to-day. This steady and undissipated attention to one object is a sure mark of a superior genius; as hurry, bustle, and agitation are the never-failing symptoms of a weak and frivolous mind. When you read Horace, attend to the justness of his thoughts, the happiness of his diction, and the beauty of his poetry; and do not think of Puffendorf de Homine el Cive; and, when you are reading Puffendorf, do not think of Madame de St. Germain; nor of Puffendorf, when you are talking to Madame de St. Germain.

Mr. Harte informs me, that he has reimbursed you of part of your losses in Germany; and I consent to his reimbursing you of the whole, now that I know you deserve it. I shall grudge you nothing, nor shall you want anything that you desire, provided you deserve it; so that you see, it is in your own power to have whatever you please.

There is a little book which you read here with Monsieur Codere entitled, 'Maniere de bien penser dans les Ouvrages d'Esprit,' written by Pyre Bonhours. I wish you would read this book again at your leisure hours, for it will not only divert you, but likewise form your taste, and give you a just manner of thinking. Adieu!

LETTER X

London, June 30, O. S. 1747

Dear boy: I was extremely pleased with the account which you gave me in your last, of the civilities that you received in your Swiss progress; and I have written, by this post, to Mr. Burnaby, and to the 'Avoyer,' to thank them for their parts. If the attention you met with pleased you, as I dare say it did, you will, I hope, draw this general conclusion from it, that attention and civility please all those to whom they are paid; and that you will please others in proportion as you are attentive and civil to them.

Bishop Burnet has wrote his travels through Switzerland; and Mr. Stanyan, from a long residence there, has written the best account, yet extant, of the Thirteen Cantons; but those books will be read no more, I presume, after you shall have published your account of that country. I hope you will favor me with one of the first copies. To be serious; though I do not desire that you should immediately turn author, and oblige the world with your travels; yet, wherever you go, I would have you as curious and inquisitive as if you did intend to write them. I do not mean that you should give yourself so much trouble, to know the number of houses, inhabitants, signposts, and tombstones, of every town that you go through; but that you should inform yourself, as well as your stay will permit you, whether the town is free, or to whom it belongs, or in what manner: whether it has any peculiar privileges or customs; what trade or manufactures; and such other particulars as people of sense desire to know. And there would be no manner of harm if you were to take memorandums of such things in a paper book to help your memory. The only way of knowing all these things is to keep the best company, who can best inform you of them. I am just now called away; so good night.

LETTER XI

London, July 20, O. S. 1747

Dear boy: In your Mamma's letter, which goes here inclosed, you will find one from my sister, to thank you for the Arquebusade water which you sent her; and which she takes very kindly. She would not show me her letter to you; but told me that it contained good wishes and good advice; and, as I know she will show your letter in answer to hers, I send you here inclosed the draught of the letter which I would have you write to her. I hope you will not be offended at my offering you my assistance upon this occasion; because, I presume, that as yet, you are not much used to write to ladies. 'A propos' of letter-writing, the best models that you can form yourself upon are, Cicero, Cardinal d'Ossat, Madame Sevigne, and Comte Bussy Rebutin. Cicero's Epistles to Atticus, and to his familiar friends, are the best examples that you can imitate, in the friendly and the familiar style. The simplicity and the clearness of Cardinal d'Ossat's letters show how letters of business ought to be written; no affected turns, no attempts at wit, obscure or perplex his matter; which is always plainly and clearly stated, as business always should be. For gay and amusing letters, for 'enjouement and badinage,' there are none that equal Comte Bussy's and Madame Sevigne's. They are so natural, that they seem to be the extempore conversations of two people of wit, rather, than letters which are commonly studied, though they ought not to be so. I would advise you to let that book be one in your itinerant library; it will both amuse and inform you.

I have not time to add any more now; so good night.

LETTER XII

London, July 30, O. S. 1747

Dear boy: It is now four posts since I have received any letter, either from you or from Mr. Harte. I impute this to the rapidity of your travels through Switzerland; which I suppose are by this time finished.

You will have found by my late letters, both to you and Mr. Harte, that you are to be at Leipsig by next Michaelmas; where you will be lodged in the house of Professor Mascow, and boarded in the neighborhood of it, with some young men of fashion. The professor will read you lectures upon 'Grotius de Jure Belli et Pacis,' the 'Institutes of Justinian' and the 'Jus Publicum Imperii;' which I expect that you shall not only hear, but attend to, and retain. I also expect that you make yourself perfectly master of the German language; which you may very soon do there, if you please. I give you fair warning, that at Leipsig I shall have an hundred invisible spies about you; and shall be exactly informed of everything that you do, and of almost everything that you say. I hope that, in consequence of those minute informations, I may be able to say of you, what Velleius Paterculus says of Scipio; that in his whole life, 'nihil non laudandum aut dixit, aut fecit, aut sensit.' There is a great deal of good company in Leipsig, which I would have you frequent in the evenings, when the studies of the day are over. There is likewise a kind of court kept there, by a Duchess Dowager of Courland; at which you should get introduced. The King of Poland and his Court go likewise to the fair at Leipsig twice a year; and I shall write to Sir Charles Williams, the king's minister there, to have you presented, and introduced into good company. But I must remind you, at the same time, that it will be to a very little purpose for you to frequent good company, if you do not conform to, and learn their manners; if you are not attentive to please, and well bred, with the easiness of a man of fashion. As you must attend to your manners, so you must not neglect your person; but take care to be very clean, well dressed, and genteel; to have no disagreeable attitudes, nor awkward tricks; which many people use themselves to, and then cannot leave them off. Do you take care to keep your teeth very clean, by washing them constantly every morning, and after every meal? This is very necessary, both to preserve your teeth a great while, and to save you a great deal of pain. Mine have plagued me long, and are now falling out, merely from want of care when I was your age. Do you dress well, and not too well? Do you consider your air and manner of presenting yourself enough, and not too much? Neither negligent nor stiff? All these things deserve a degree of care, a second-rate attention; they give an additional lustre to real merit. My Lord Bacon says, that a pleasing figure is a perpetual letter of recommendation. It is certainly an agreeable forerunner of merit, and smoothes the way for it.

Remember that I shall see you at Hanover next summer, and shall expect perfection; which if I do not meet with, or at least something very near it, you and I shall, not be very well together. I shall dissect and analyze you with a microscope; so that I shall discover the least speck or blemish. This is fair warning; therefore take your measures accordingly. Yours.

LETTER XIII

London, August 21, O. S. 1747.

Dear boy: I reckon that this letter has but a bare chance of finding you at Lausanne; but I was resolved to risk it, as it is the last that I shall write to you till you are settled at Leipsig. I sent you by the last post, under cover to Mr. Harte, a letter of recommendation to one of the first people at Munich; which you will take care to present to him in the politest manner; he will certainly have you presented to the electoral family; and I hope you will go through that ceremony with great respect, good breeding, and ease. As this is the first court that ever you will have been at, take care to inform yourself if there be any particular, customs or forms to be observed, that you may not commit any mistake. At Vienna men always make courtesies, instead of bows, to the emperor; in France nobody bows at all to the king, nor kisses his hand; but in Spain and England, bows are made, and hands are kissed. Thus every court has some peculiarity or other, of which those who go to them ought previously to inform themselves, to avoid blunders and awkwardnesses.

I have not time to say any more now, than to wish you good journey to Leipsig; and great attention, both there and in going there. Adieu.

LETTER XIV

London, September 21, O. S. 1747

Dear boy: I received, by the last post, your letter of the 8th, N. S., and I do not wonder that you are surprised at the credulity and superstition of the Papists at Einsiedlen, and at their absurd stories of their chapel. But remember, at the same time, that errors and mistakes, however gross, in matters of opinion, if they are sincere, are to be pitied, but not punished nor laughed at. The blindness of the understanding is as much to be pitied as the blindness of the eye; and there is neither jest nor guilt in a man's losing his way in either case. Charity bids us set him right if we can, by arguments and persuasions; but charity, at the same time, forbids, either to punish or ridicule his misfortune. Every man's reason is, and must be, his guide; and I may as well expect that every man should be of my size and complexion, as that he should reason just as I do. Every man seeks for truth; but God only knows who has found it. It is, therefore, as unjust to persecute, as it is absurd to ridicule, people for those several opinions, which they cannot help entertaining upon the conviction of their reason. It is the man who tells, or who acts a lie, that is guilty, and not he who honestly and sincerely believes the lie. I really know nothing more criminal, more mean, and more ridiculous than lying. It is the production either of malice, cowardice, or vanity; and generally misses of its aim in every one of these views; for lies are always detected sooner or later. If I tell a malicious lie, in order to affect any man's fortune or character, I may indeed injure him for some time; but I shall be sure to be the greatest sufferer myself at last; for as soon as ever I am detected (and detected I most certainly shall be), I am blasted for the infamous attempt; and whatever is said afterward, to the disadvantage of that person, however true, passes for calumny. If I lie, or equivocate (for it is the same thing), in order to excuse myself for something that I have said or done, and to avoid the danger and the shame that I apprehend from it, I discover at once my fear as well as my falsehood; and only increase, instead of avoiding, the danger and the shame; I show myself to be the lowest and the meanest of mankind, and am sure to be always treated as such. Fear, instead of avoiding, invites danger; for concealed cowards will insult known ones. If one has had the misfortune to be in the wrong, there is something noble in frankly owning it; it is the only way of atoning for it, and the only way of being forgiven. Equivocating, evading, shuffling, in order to remove a present danger or inconveniency, is something so mean, and betrays so much fear, that whoever practices them always deserves to be, and often will be kicked. There is another sort of lies, inoffensive enough in themselves, but wonderfully ridiculous; I mean those lies which a mistaken vanity suggests, that defeat the very end for which they are calculated, and terminate in the humiliation and confusion of their author, who is sure to be detected. These are chiefly narrative and historical lies, all intended to do infinite honor to their author. He is always the hero of his own romances; he has been in dangers from which nobody but himself ever escaped; he has seen with his own eyes, whatever other people have heard or read of: he has had more 'bonnes fortunes' than ever he knew women; and has ridden more miles post in one day, than ever courier went in two. He is soon discovered, and as soon becomes the object of universal contempt and ridicule. Remember, then, as long as you live, that nothing but strict truth can carry you through the world, with either your conscience or your honor unwounded. It is not only your duty, but your interest; as a proof of which you may always observe, that the greatest fools are the greatest liars. For my own part, I judge of every man's truth by his degree of understanding.

This letter will, I suppose, find you at Leipsig; where I expect and require from you attention and accuracy, in both which you have hitherto been very deficient. Remember that I shall see you in the summer; shall examine you most narrowly; and will never forget nor forgive those faults, which it has been in your own power to prevent or cure; and be assured that I have many eyes upon you at Leipsig, besides Mr. Harte's. Adieu!

LETTER XV

London, October 2, O. S. 1747

Dear boy: By your letter of the 18th past, N. S., I find that you are a tolerably good landscape painter, and can present the several views of Switzerland to the curious. I am very glad of it, as it is a proof of some attention; but I hope you will be as good a portrait painter, which is a much more noble science. By portraits, you will easily judge, that I do not mean the outlines and the coloring of the human figure; but the inside of the heart and mind of man. This science requires more attention, observation, and penetration, than the other; as indeed it is infinitely more useful. Search, therefore, with the greatest care, into the characters of those whom you converse with; endeavor to discover their predominant passions, their prevailing weaknesses, their vanities, their follies, and their humors, with all the right and wrong, wise and silly springs of human actions, which make such inconsistent and whimsical beings of us rational creatures. A moderate share of penetration, with great attention, will infallibly make these necessary discoveries. This is the true knowledge of the world; and the world is a country which nobody ever yet knew by description; one must travel through it one's self to be acquainted with it. The scholar, who in the dust of his closet talks or writes of the world, knows no more of it, than that orator did of war, who judiciously endeavored to instruct Hannibal in it. Courts and camps are the only places to learn the world in. There alone all kinds of characters resort, and human nature is seen in all the various shapes and modes, which education, custom, and habit give it; whereas, in all other places, one local mode generally prevails, and producing a seeming though not a real sameness of character. For example, one general mode distinguishes an university, another a trading town, a third a seaport town, and so on; whereas, at a capital, where the Prince or the Supreme Power resides, some of all these various modes are to be seen and seen in action too, exerting their utmost skill in pursuit of their several objects. Human nature is the same all over the world; but its operations are so varied by education and habit, that one must see it in all its dresses in order to be intimately acquainted with it. The passion of ambition, for instance, is the same in a courtier, a soldier, or an ecclesiastic; but, from their different educations and habits, they will take very different methods to gratify it. Civility, which is a disposition to accommodate and oblige others, is essentially the same in every country; but goodbreeding, as it is called, which is the manner of exerting that disposition, is different in almost every country, and merely local; and every man of sense imitates and conforms to that local good-breeding of the place which he is at. A conformity and flexibility of manners is necessary in the course of the world; that is, with regard to all things which are not wrong in themselves. The 'versatile ingenium' is the most useful of all. It can turn itself instantly from one object to another, assuming the proper manner for each. It can be serious with the grave, cheerful with the gay, and trifling with the frivolous. Endeavor by all means, to acquire this talent, for it is a very great one.

As I hardly know anything more useful, than to see, from time to time, pictures of one's self drawn by different hands, I send you here a sketch of yourself, drawn at

Lausanne, while you were there, and sent over here by a person who little thought that it would ever fall into my hands: and indeed it was by the greatest accident in the world that it did.

LETTER XVI

London, October 9, O. S. 1747.

Dear boy: People of your age have, commonly, an unguarded frankness about them; which makes them the easy prey and bubbles of the artful and the experienced; they look upon every knave or fool, who tells them that he is their friend, to be really so; and pay that profession of simulated friendship, with an indiscreet and unbounded confidence, always to their loss, often to their ruin. Beware, therefore, now that you are coming into the world, of these preferred friendships. Receive them with great civility, but with great incredulity too; and pay them with compliments, but not with confidence. Do not let your vanity and self-love make you suppose that people become your friends at first sight, or even upon a short acquaintance. Real friendship is a slow grower and never thrives unless engrafted upon a stock of known and reciprocal merit. There is another kind of nominal friendship among young people, which is warm for the time, but by good luck, of short duration. This friendship is hastily produced, by their being accidentally thrown together, and pursuing the course of riot and debauchery. A fine friendship, truly; and well cemented by drunkenness and lewdness. It should rather be called a conspiracy against morals and good manners, and be punished as such by the civil magistrate. However, they have the impudence and folly to call this confederacy a friendship. They lend one another money, for bad purposes; they engage in quarrels, offensive and defensive for their accomplices; they tell one another all they know, and often more too, when, of a sudden, some accident disperses them, and they think no more of each other, unless it be to betray and laugh, at their imprudent confidence. Remember to make a great difference between companions and friends; for a very complaisant and agreeable companion may, and often does, prove a very improper and a very dangerous friend. People will, in a great degree, and not without reason, form their opinion of you, upon that which they have of your friends; and there is a Spanish proverb, which says very justly, *tell me who you live with and* I *will tell you who you are*. One may fairly suppose, that the man who makes a knave or a fool his friend, has something very bad to do or to conceal. But, at the same time that you carefully decline the friendship of knaves and fools, if it can be called friendship, there is no occasion to make either of them your enemies, wantonly and unprovoked; for they are numerous bodies: and I, would rather choose a secure neutrality, than alliance, or war with either of them. You may be a declared enemy to their vices and follies, without being marked out by them as a personal one. Their enmity is the next dangerous thing to their friendship. Have a real reserve with almost everybody; and have a seeming reserve with almost nobody; for it is very disagreeable to seem reserved, and very dangerous not to be so. Few people find the true medium; many are ridiculously mysterious and reserved upon trifles; and many imprudently communicative of all they know.

The next thing to the choice of your friends, is the choice of your company. Endeavor, as much as you can, to keep company with people above you: there you rise, as much as you sink with people below you; for (as I have mentioned before) you are whatever the company you keep is. Do not mistake, when I say company above you, and think that I mean with regard to, their birth: that is the least consideration; but I mean with regard to their merit, and the light in which the world considers them.

There are two sorts of good company; one, which is called the beau monde, and consists of the people who have the lead in courts, and in the gay parts of life; the other consists of those who are distinguished by some peculiar merit, or who excel in some particular and valuable art or science. For my own part, I used to think myself in company as, much above me, when I was with Mr. Addison and Mr. Pope, as if I had been with all the princes in Europe. What I mean by low company, which should by all means be avoided, is the company of those, who, absolutely insignificant and contemptible in themselves, think they are honored by being in your company; and who flatter every vice and every folly you have, in order to engage you to converse with them. The pride of being the first of the company is but too common; but it is very silly, and very prejudicial. Nothing in the world lets down a character quicker than that wrong turn.

You may possibly ask me, whether a man has it always in his power to get the best company? and how? I say, Yes, he has, by deserving it; providing he is but in circumstances which enable him to appear upon the footing of a gentleman. Merit and good-breeding will make their way everywhere. Knowledge will introduce him, and good-breeding will endear him to the best companies: for, as I have often told you, politeness and good-breeding are absolutely necessary to adorn any, or all other good qualities or talents. Without them, no knowledge, no perfection whatever, is seen in its best light. The scholar, without good-breeding, is a pedant; the philosopher, a cynic; the soldier, a brute; and every man disagreeable.

I long to hear, from my several correspondents at Leipsig, of your arrival there, and what impression you make on them at first; for I have Arguses, with an hundred eyes each, who will watch you narrowly, and relate to me faithfully. My accounts will certainly be true; it depends upon you, entirely, of what kind they shall be. Adieu.

LETTER XVII

London, October 16, O. S. 1747

Dear boy: The art of pleasing is a very necessary one to possess; but a very difficult one to acquire. It can hardly be reduced to rules; and your own good sense and observation will teach you more of it than I can. Do as you would be done by, is the surest method that I know of pleasing. Observe carefully what pleases you in others, and probably the same thing in you will please others. If you are pleased with the complaisance and attention of others to your humors, your tastes, or your weaknesses, depend upon it the same complaisance and attention, on your part to theirs, will equally please them. Take the tone of the company that you are in, and do not pretend to give it; be serious, gay, or even trifling, as you find the present humor of the company; this is an attention due from every individual to the majority. Do not tell stories in company; there is nothing more tedious and disagreeable; if by chance you know a very short story, and exceedingly applicable to the present subject of conversation, tell it in as few words as possible; and even then, throw out that you do not love to tell stories; but that the shortness of it tempted you. Of all things, banish the egotism out of your conversation, and never think of entertaining people with your own personal concerns, or private, affairs; though they are interesting to you, they are tedious and impertinent to everybody else; besides that, one cannot keep one's own private affairs too secret. Whatever you think your own excellencies may be, do not affectedly display them in company; nor labor, as many people do, to give that turn to the conversation, which may supply you with an opportunity of exhibiting them. If they are real, they will infallibly be discovered, without your pointing them out yourself, and with much more advantage. Never maintain an argument with heat and clamor, though you think or know yourself to be in the right: but give your opinion modestly and coolly, which is the only way to convince; and, if that does not do, try to change the conversation, by saying, with good humor, "We shall hardly convince one another, nor is it necessary that we should, so let us talk of something else."

Remember that there is a local propriety to be observed in all companies; and that what is extremely proper in one company, may be, and often is, highly improper in another.

The jokes, the 'bonmots,' the little adventures, which may do very well in one company, will seem flat and tedious, when related in another. The particular characters, the habits, the cant of one company, may give merit to a word, or a gesture, which would have none at all if divested of those accidental circumstances. Here people very commonly err; and fond of something that has entertained them in one company, and in certain circumstances, repeat it with emphasis in another, where it is either insipid, or, it may be, offensive, by being ill-timed or misplaced. Nay, they often do it with this silly preamble; "I will tell you an excellent thing"; or, "I will tell you the best thing in the world." This raises expectations, which, when absolutely disappointed, make the relater of this excellent thing look, very deservedly, like a fool.

If you would particularly gain the affection and friendship of particular people, whether men or women, endeavor to find out the predominant excellency, if they have one, and their prevailing weakness, which everybody has; and do justice to the one, and something more than justice to the other. Men have various objects in which they may excel, or at least would be thought to excel; and, though they love to hear justice done to them, where they know that they excel, yet they are most and best flattered upon those points where they wish to excel, and yet are doubtful whether they do or not. As, for example, Cardinal Richelieu, who was undoubtedly the ablest statesman of his time, or perhaps of any other, had the idle vanity of being thought the best poet too; he envied the great Corneille his reputation, and ordered a criticism to be written upon the "Cid." Those, therefore, who flattered skillfully, said little to him of his abilities in state affairs, or at least but 'en passant,' and as it might naturally occur. But the incense which they gave him, the smoke of which they knew would turn his head in their favor, was as a 'bel esprit' and a poet. Why? Because he was sure of one excellency, and distrustful as to the other. You will easily discover every man's prevailing vanity, by observing his favorite topic of conversation; for every man talks most of what he has most a mind to be thought to excel in. Touch him but there, and you touch him to the quick. The late Sir Robert Walpole (who was certainly an able man) was little open to flattery upon that head; for he was in no doubt himself about it; but his prevailing weakness was, to be thought to have a polite and happy turn to gallantry; of which he had undoubtedly less than any man living: it was his favorite and frequent subject of conversation: which proved, to those who had any penetration, that it was his prevailing weakness. And they applied to it with success.

Women have, in general, but one object, which is their beauty; upon which, scarce any flattery is too gross for them to swallow. Nature has hardly formed a woman ugly enough to be insensible to flattery upon her person; if her face is so shocking, that she must in some degree, be conscious of it, her figure and her air, she trusts, make ample amends for it. If her figure is deformed, her face, she thinks, counterbalances it. If they are both bad, she comforts herself that she has graces; a certain manner; a 'je ne sais quoi,' still more engaging than beauty. This truth is evident, from the studied and elaborate dress of the ugliest women in the world. An undoubted, uncontested, conscious beauty, is of all women, the least sensible of flattery upon that head; she knows that it is her due, and is therefore obliged to nobody for giving it her. She must be flattered upon her understanding; which, though she may possibly not doubt of herself, yet she suspects that men may distrust.

Do not mistake me, and think that I mean to recommend to you abject and criminal flattery: no; flatter nobody's vices or crimes: on the contrary, abhor and discourage them. But there is no living in the world without a complaisant indulgence for people's weaknesses, and innocent, though ridiculous vanities. If a man has a mind to be thought wiser, and a woman handsomer than they really are, their error is a comfortable one to themselves, and an innocent one with regard to other people; and I would rather make them my friends, by indulging them in it, than my enemies, by endeavoring (and that to no purpose) to undeceive them.

There are little attentions likewise, which are infinitely engaging, and which sensibly affect that degree of pride and self-love, which is inseparable from human nature; as they are unquestionable proofs of the regard and consideration which we have for the person to whom we pay them. As, for example, to observe the little habits, the likings, the antipathies, and the tastes of those whom we would gain; and then take care to provide them with the one, and to secure them from the other; giving them, genteelly, to understand, that you had observed that they liked such a dish, or such a room; for which reason you had prepared it: or, on the contrary, that having observed they had an aversion to such a dish, a dislike to such a person, *etc.*, you had taken care to avoid presenting them. Such attention to such trifles flatters self-love much more than greater things, as it makes people think themselves almost the only objects of your thoughts and care.

These are some of the arcana necessary for your initiation in the great society of the world. I wish I had known them better at your age; I have paid the price of three-and-fifty years for them, and shall not grudge it, if you reap the advantage. Adieu.

LETTER XVIII

London, October 30, O. S. 1747

Dear boy: I am very well pleased with your 'Itinerarium,' which you sent me from Ratisbon. It shows me that you observe and inquire as you go, which is the true end of traveling. Those who travel heedlessly from place to place, observing only their distance from each other, and attending only to their accommodation at the inn at night, set out fools, and will certainly return so. Those who only mind the raree-shows of the places which they go through, such as steeples, clocks, town-houses, *etc.*, get so little by their travels, that they might as well stay at home. But those who observe, and inquire into the situations, the strength, the weakness, the trade, the manufactures, the government, and constitution of every place they go to; who frequent the best companies, and attend to their several manners and characters; those alone travel with advantage; and as they set out wise, return wiser.

I would advise you always to get the shortest description or history of every place where you make any stay; and such a book, however imperfect, will still suggest to you matter for inquiry; upon which you may get better informations from the people of the place. For example; while you are at Leipsig, get some short account (and to be sure there are many such) of the present state of the town, with regard to its magistrates, its police, its privileges, *etc.*, and then inform yourself more minutely upon all those heads in, conversation with the most intelligent people. Do the same thing afterward with regard to the Electorate of Saxony: you will find a short history of it in Puffendorf's Introduction, which will give you a general idea of it, and point out to you the proper objects of a more minute inquiry. In short, be curious, attentive, inquisitive, as to everything; listlessness and indolence are always blameable, but, at your age, they are unpardonable. Consider how precious, and how important for all the rest of your life, are your moments for these next three or four years; and do not lose one of them. Do not think I mean that you should study all day long; I am far from advising or desiring it: but I desire that you would be doing something or other all day long; and not neglect half hours and quarters of hours, which, at the, year's end, amount to a great sum. For instance, there are many short intervals during the day, between studies and pleasures: instead of sitting idle and yawning, in those intervals, take up any book, though ever so trifling a one, even down to a jest-book; it is still better than doing nothing.

Nor do I call pleasures idleness, or time lost, provided they are the pleasures of a rational being; on the contrary, a certain portion of your time, employed in those pleasures, is very usefully employed. Such are public spectacles, assemblies of good company, cheerful suppers, and even balls; but then, these require attention, or else your time is quite lost.

There are a great many people, who think themselves employed all day, and who, if they were to cast up their accounts at night, would find that they had done just nothing. They have read two or three hours mechanically, without attending to what they read, and consequently without either retaining it, or reasoning upon it. From thence they saunter into company, without taking any part in it, and without observing the characters of the persons, or the subjects of the conversation; but are either thinking of some trifle, foreign to the present purpose, or often not thinking at all; which silly and idle suspension of thought they would dignify with the name of *absence* and *distraction*. They go afterward, it may be, to the play, where they gape at the company and the lights; but without minding the very thing they went to, the play.

Pray do you be as attentive to your pleasures as to your studies. In the latter, observe and reflect upon all you read; and, in the former, be watchful and attentive to all that you see and hear; and never have it to say, as a thousand fools do, of things that were said and done before their faces, that, truly, they did not mind them, because they were thinking of something else. Why were they thinking of something else? and if they were, why did they come there? The truth is, that the fools were thinking of nothing. Remember the 'hoc age,' do what you are about, be what it will; it is either worth doing well, or not at all. Wherever you are, have (as the low vulgar expression is) your ears and your eyes about you. Listen to everything that is said, and see everything that is done. Observe the looks and countenances of those who speak, which is often a surer way of discovering the truth than from what they say. But then keep all those observations to yourself, for your own private use, and rarely communicate them to others. Observe, without being thought an observer, for otherwise people will be upon their guard before you.

Consider seriously, and follow carefully, I beseech you, my dear child, the advice which from time to time I have given, and shall continue to give you; it is at once the result of my long experience, and the effect of my tenderness for you. I can have no interest in it but yours. You are not yet capable of wishing yourself half so well as I wish you; follow therefore, for a time at least, implicitly, advice which you cannot suspect, though possibly you may not yet see the particular advantages of it; but you will one day feel them. Adieu.

LETTER XIX

London, November 6, O. S. 1747

Dear boy: Three mails are now due from Holland, so that I have no letter from you to acknowledge; I write to you, therefore, now, as usual, by way of flapper, to put you in mind of yourself. Doctor Swift, in his account of the island of Laputa, describes some philosophers there who were so wrapped up and absorbed in their abstruse speculations, that they would have forgotten all the common and necessary duties of life, if they had not been reminded of them by persons who flapped them, whenever they observed them continue too long in any of those learned trances. I do not indeed suspect you of being absorbed in abstruse speculations; but, with great submission to you, may I not suspect that levity, inattention, and too little thinking, require a flapper, as well as too deep thinking? If my letters should happen to get to you when you are sitting by the fire and doing nothing, or when you are gaping at the window, may they not be very proper flaps, to put you in mind that you might employ your time much better? I knew once a very covetous, sordid fellow, who used frequently to say, "Take care of the pence; for the pounds will take care of themselves." This was a just and sensible reflection in a miser. I recommend to you to take care of the minutes; for hours will take care of themselves. I am very sure, that many people lose two or three hours every day, by not taking care of the minutes. Never think any portion of time whatsoever too short to be employed; something or other may always be done in it.

While you are in Germany, let all your historical studies be relative to Germany; not only the general history of the empire as a collective body; but the respective electorates, principalities, and towns; and also the genealogy of the most considerable families. A genealogy is no trifle in Germany; and they would rather prove their two-and-thirty quarters, than two-and-thirty cardinal virtues, if there were so many. They are not of Ulysses' opinion, who says very truly,

 ———Genus et proavos, et qua non fecimus ipsi;
 Vix ea nostra voco.

Good night.

LETTER XX

London, November 24, O. S. 1747

Dear boy: As often as I write to you (and that you know is pretty often), so often I am in doubt whether it is to any purpose, and whether it is not labor and paper lost. This entirely depends upon the degree of reason and reflection which you are master of, or think proper to exert. If you give yourself time to think, and have sense enough to think right, two reflections must necessarily occur to you; the one is, that I have a great deal of experience, and that you have none: the other is, that I am the only man living who cannot have, directly or indirectly, any interest concerning you, but your own. From which two undeniable principles, the obvious and necessary conclusion is, that you ought, for your own sake, to attend to and follow my advice.

If, by the application which I recommend to you, you acquire great knowledge, you alone are the gainer; I pay for it. If you should deserve either a good or a bad character, mine will be exactly what it is now, and will neither be the better in the first case, nor worse in the latter. You alone will be the gainer or the loser.

Whatever your pleasures may be, I neither can nor shall envy you them, as old people are sometimes suspected by young people to do; and I shall only lament, if they should prove such as are unbecoming a man of honor, or below a man of sense. But you will be the real sufferer, if they are such. As therefore, it is plain that I can have no other motive than that of affection in whatever I say to you, you ought to look upon me as your best, and, for some years to come, your only friend.

True friendship requires certain proportions of age and manners, and can never subsist where they are extremely different, except in the relations of parent and child, where affection on one side, and regard on the other, make up the difference. The friendship which you may contract with people of your own age may be sincere, may be warm; but must be, for some time, reciprocally unprofitable, as there can be no experience on either side. The young leading the young, is like the blind leading the blind; (they will both fall into the ditch.) The only sure guide is, he who has often gone the road which you want to go. Let me be that guide; who have gone all roads, and who can consequently point out to you the best. If you ask me why I went any of the bad roads myself, I will answer you very truly, That it was for want of a good guide: ill example invited me one way, and a good guide was wanting to show me a better. But if anybody, capable of advising me, had taken the same pains with me, which I have taken, and will continue to take with you, I should have avoided many follies and inconveniences, which undirected youth run me into. My father was neither desirous nor able to advise me; which is what, I hope, you cannot say of yours. You see that I make use, only of the word advice; because I would much rather have the assent of your reason to my advice, than the submission of your will to my, authority. This, I persuade myself, will happen, from that degree of sense which I think you have; and therefore I will go on advising, and with hopes of success.

You are now settled for some time at Leipsig; the principal object of your stay there is the knowledge of books and sciences; which if you do not, by attention and application, make yourself master of while you are there, you will be ignorant of them all the rest of your life; and, take my word for it, a life of ignorance is not only a very contemptible, but a very tiresome one. Redouble your attention, then, to Mr. Harte, in your private studies of the 'Literae Humaniores,' especially Greek. State your difficulties, whenever you have any; and do not suppress them, either from mistaken shame, lazy indifference, or in order to have done the sooner. Do the same when you are at lectures with Professor Mascow, or any other professor; let nothing pass till you are sure that you understand it thoroughly; and accustom yourself to write down the capital points of what you learn. When you have thus usefully employed your mornings, you may, with a safe conscience, divert yourself in the evenings, and make those evenings very useful too, by passing them in good company, and, by observation and attention, learning as much of the world as Leipsig can teach you. You will observe and imitate the manners of the people of the best fashion there; not that they are (it may be) the best manners in the world; but because they are the best manners of the place where you are, to which a man of sense always conforms. The nature of things (as I have often told you) is always and everywhere the same; but the modes of them vary more or less, in every country; and an easy and genteel conformity to them, or rather the assuming of them at proper times, and in proper places, is what particularly constitutes a man of the world, and a well-bred man.

Here is advice enough, I think, and too much, it may be, you will think, for one letter; if you follow it, you will get knowledge, character, and pleasure by it; if you do not, I only lose 'operam et oleum,' which, in all events, I do not grudge you.

I send you, by a person who sets out this day for Leipsig, a small packet from your Mamma, containing some valuable things which you left behind, to which I have added, by way of new-year's gift, a very pretty tooth-pick case; and, by the way, pray take great care of your teeth, and keep them extremely clean. I have likewise sent you the Greek roots, lately translated into English from the French of the Port Royal. Inform yourself what the Port Royal is. To conclude with a quibble: I hope you will not only feed upon these Greek roots, but likewise digest them perfectly. Adieu.

LETTER XXI

London, December 15, O. S. 1747

Dear Boy: There is nothing which I more wish that you should know, and which fewer people do know, than the true use and value of time. It is in everybody's mouth; but in few people's practice. Every fool, who slatterns away his whole time in nothings, utters, however, some trite commonplace sentence, of which there are millions, to prove, at once, the value and the fleetness of time. The sun-dials, likewise all over Europe, have some ingenious inscription to that effect; so that nobody squanders away their time, without hearing and seeing, daily, how necessary it is to employ it well, and how irrecoverable it is if lost. But all these admonitions are useless, where there is not a fund of good sense and reason to suggest them, rather than receive them. By the manner in which you now tell me that you employ your time, I flatter myself that you have that fund; that is the fund which will make you rich indeed. I do not, therefore, mean to give you a critical essay upon the use and abuse of time; but I will only give you some hints with regard to the use of one particular period of that long time which, I hope, you have before you; I mean, the next two years. Remember, then, that whatever knowledge you do not solidly lay the foundation of before you are eighteen, you will never be the master of while you breathe. Knowledge is a comfortable and necessary retreat and shelter for us in an advanced age; and if we do not plant it while young, it will give us no shade when we grow old. I neither require nor expect from you great application to books, after you are once thrown out into the great world. I know it is impossible; and it may even, in some cases, be improper; this, therefore, is your time, and your only time, for unwearied and uninterrupted application. If you should sometimes think it a little laborious, consider that labor is the unavoidable fatigue of a necessary journey. The more hours a day you travel, the sooner you will be at your journey's end. The sooner you are qualified for your liberty, the sooner you shall have it; and your manumission will entirely depend upon the manner in which you employ the intermediate time. I think I offer you a very good bargain, when I promise you, upon my word, that if you will do everything that I would have you do, till you are eighteen, I will do everything that you would have me do ever afterward.

I knew a gentleman, who was so good a manager of his time, that he would not even lose that small portion of it, which the calls of nature obliged him to pass in the necessary-house; but gradually went through all the Latin poets, in those moments. He bought, for example, a common edition of Horace, of which he tore off gradually a couple of pages, carried them with him to that necessary place, read them first, and then sent them down as a sacrifice to Cloacina: this was so much time fairly gained; and I recommend you to follow his example. It is better than only doing what you cannot help doing at those moments; and it will made any book, which you shall read in that manner, very present in your mind. Books of science, and of a grave sort, must be read with continuity; but there are very many, and even very useful ones, which may be read with advantage by snatches, and unconnectedly; such are all the good Latin poets, except Virgil in his "AEneid": and such are most of the modern poets, in which you will find many pieces worth reading, that will not take up above

37

seven or eight minutes. Bayle's, Moreri's, and other dictionaries, are proper books to take and shut up for the little intervals of (otherwise) idle time, that everybody has in the course of the day, between either their studies or their pleasures. Good night.

LETTER XXII

London, December 18, O. S. 1747.

Dear Boy: As two mails are now due from Holland,

I have no letters of yours, or Mr. Harte's to acknowledge; so that this letter is the effect of that 'scribendi cacoethes,' which my fears, my hopes, and my doubts, concerning you give me. When I have wrote you a very long letter upon any subject, it is no sooner gone, but I think I have omitted something in it, which might be of use to you; and then I prepare the supplement for the next post: or else some new subject occurs to me, upon which I fancy I can give you some informations, or point out some rules which may be advantageous to you. This sets me to writing again, though God knows whether to any purpose or not; a few years more can only ascertain that. But, whatever my success may be, my anxiety and my care can only be the effects of that tender affection which I have for you; and which you cannot represent to yourself greater than it really is. But do not mistake the nature of that affection, and think it of a kind that you may with impunity abuse. It is not natural affection, there being in reality no such thing; for, if there were, some inward sentiment must necessarily and reciprocally discover the parent to the child, and the child to the parent, without any exterior indications, knowledge, or acquaintance whatsoever; which never happened since the creation of the world, whatever poets, romance, and novel writers, and such sentiment-mongers, may be pleased to say to the contrary. Neither is my affection for you that of a mother, of which the only, or at least the chief objects, are health and life: I wish you them both most heartily; but, at the same time, I confess they are by no means my principal care.

My object is to have you fit to live; which, if you are not, I do not desire that you should live at all. My affection for you then is, and only will be, proportioned to your merit; which is the only affection that one rational being ought to have for another. Hitherto I have discovered nothing wrong in your heart, or your head: on the contrary I think I see sense in the one, and sentiments in the other. This persuasion is the only motive of my present affection; which will either increase or diminish, according to your merit or demerit. If you have the knowledge, the honor, and probity, which you may have, the marks and warmth of my affection shall amply reward them; but if you have them not, my aversion and indignation will rise in the same proportion; and, in that case, remember, that I am under no further obligation, than to give you the necessary means of subsisting. If ever we quarrel, do not expect or depend upon any weakness in my nature, for a reconciliation, as children frequently do, and often meet with, from silly parents; I have no such weakness about me: and, as I will never quarrel with you but upon some essential point; if once we quarrel, I will never forgive. But I hope and believe, that this declaration (for it is no threat) will prove unnecessary. You are no stranger to the principles of virtue; and, surely, whoever knows virtue must love it. As for knowledge, you have already enough of it, to engage you to acquire more. The ignorant only, either despise it, or think that they have enough: those who have the most are always the

39

most desirous to have more, and know that the most they can have is, alas! but too little.

Reconsider, from time to time, and retain the friendly advice which I send you. The advantage will be all your own.

LETTER XXIII

London, December 29, O. S. 1747

Dear boy: I have received two letters from you of the 17th and 22d, N. S., by the last of which I find that some of mine to you must have miscarried; for I have never been above two posts without writing to you or to Mr. Harte, and even very long letters. I have also received a letter from Mr. Harte, which gives me great satisfaction: it is full of your praises; and he answers for you, that, in two years more, you will deserve your manumission, and be fit to go into the world, upon a footing that will do you honor, and give me pleasure.

I thank you for your offer of the new edition of 'Adamus Adami,' but I do not want it, having a good edition of it at present. When you have read that, you will do well to follow it with Pere Bougeant's 'Histoire du Traite de Munster,' in two volumes quarto; which contains many important anecdotes concerning that famous treaty, that are not in Adamus Adami.

You tell me that your lectures upon the 'Jus Publicum' will be ended at Easter; but then I hope that Monsieur Mascow will begin them again; for I would not have you discontinue that study one day while you are at Leipsig. I suppose that Monsieur Mascow will likewise give you lectures upon the 'Instrumentum Pacis,' and upon the capitulations of the late emperors. Your German will go on of course; and I take it for granted that your stay at Leipsig will make you a perfect master of that language, both as to speaking and writing; for remember, that knowing any language imperfectly, is very little better than not knowing it at all: people being as unwilling to speak in a language which they do not possess thoroughly, as others are to hear them. Your thoughts are cramped, and appear to great disadvantage, in any language of which you are not perfect master. Let modern history share part of your time, and that always accompanied with the maps of the places in question; geography and history are very imperfect separately, and, to be useful, must be joined.

Go to the Duchess of Courland's as often as she and your leisure will permit. The company of women of fashion will improve your manners, though not your understanding; and that complaisance and politeness, which are so useful in men's company, can only be acquired in women's.

Remember always, what I have told you a thousand times, that all the talents in the world will want all their lustre, and some part of their use too, if they are not adorned with that easy good-breeding, that engaging manner, and those graces, which seduce and prepossess people in your favor at first sight. A proper care of your person is by no means to be neglected; always extremely clean; upon proper occasions fine. Your carriage genteel, and your motions graceful. Take particular care of your manner and address, when you present yourself in company. Let them be respectful without meanness, easy without too much familiarity, genteel without affectation, and insinuating without any seeming art or design.

You need not send me any more extracts of the German constitution; which, by the course of your present studies, I know you must soon be acquainted with; but I would now rather that your letters should be a sort of journal of your own life. As, for instance, what company you keep, what new acquaintances you make, what your pleasures are; with your own reflections upon the whole: likewise what Greek and Latin books you read and understand. Adieu!

Attention and civility please all
Avoid singularity
Blindness of the understanding is as much to be pitied
Choose your pleasures for yourself
Civility, which is a disposition to accommodate and oblige others
Complaisant indulgence for people's weaknesses
Contempt
Disagreeable to seem reserved, and very dangerous not to be so
Do as you would be done by
Do what you are about
Dress well, and not too well
Dressed like the reasonable people of your own age
Easy without too much familiarity
Employ your whole time, which few people do
Exalt the gentle in woman and man—above the merely genteel
Eyes and ears open and mouth mostly shut
Fit to live—or not live at all
Flexibility of manners is necessary in the course of the world
Genteel without affectation
Geography and history are very imperfect separately
Good-breeding
Gratitude not being universal, nor even common
Greatest fools are the greatest liars
He that is gentil doeth gentil deeds
If once we quarrel, I will never forgive
Injury is much sooner forgotten than an insult
Judge of every man's truth by his degree of understanding
Knowing any language imperfectly
Knowledge: either despise it, or think that they have enough
Labor is the unavoidable fatigue of a necessary journey
Let nothing pass till you understand it
Life of ignorance is not only a very contemptible, but tiresome
Listlessness and indolence are always blameable
Make a great difference between companions and friends
Make himself whatever he pleases, except a good poet
Merit and good-breeding will make their way everywhere
Never maintain an argument with heat and clamor
Observe, without being thought an observer
Only doing one thing at a time
Pay them with compliments, but not with confidence
Pleasure is the rock which most young people split upon

Pride of being the first of the company
Real friendship is a slow grower
Receive them with great civility, but with great incredulity
Recommend it(pleasure) to you, like an Epicurean
Respectful without meanness, easy without too much familiarity
Scarce any flattery is too gross for them to swallow
Sentiment-mongers
State your difficulties, whenever you have any
Studied and elaborate dress of the ugliest women in the world
Sure guide is, he who has often gone the road which you want to
Talk of natural affection is talking nonsense
tell me who you live with and I *will tell you who you are*
Thing so precious as time, and so irrecoverable when lost
True use and value of time
Unguarded frankness
Whatever is worth doing at all, is worth doing well
Wrapped up and absorbed in their abstruse speculations
Young leading the young, is like the blind leading the blind